What a Bee Can See

by Shirley Frederick
illustrated by Francesco Santalucia

Harcourt

Orlando   Boston   Dallas   Chicago   San Diego

Visit *The Learning Site!*

www.harcourtschool.com

This is a wild bee. Its home
is in a hole in a tree.

2

The bee has left its home.
It looks for some food.

A bee has big eyes. They
help the bee find nectar.

4

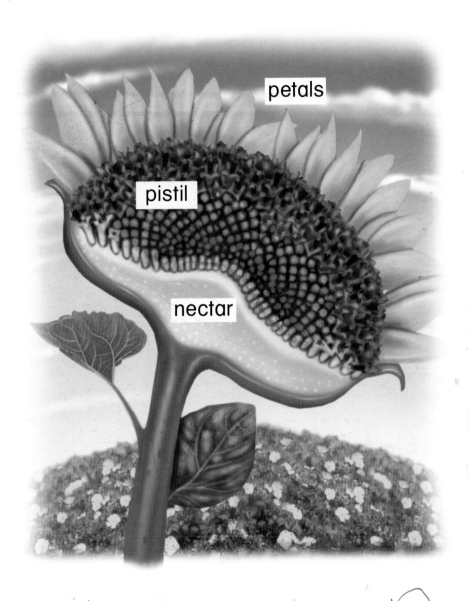

petals

pistil

nectar

Nectar is sweet water inside a flower.

The flowers in this field are green. The bee does not like these flowers.

This wild flower is red, but
the bee does not see red.

Here is another field. The bee can see most of these flowers.

The bee drinks the nectar from the yellow and blue flowers.

The bee goes home to tell
the other bees about this
field.

Many bees will go to the wild
flowers and get the nectar.

This is what a bee sees in
this field. Bees know where
the nectar is!